WHAT'S IT LIKE TO BE A...?

ANIMATOR

Elizabeth Dowen   Lisa Thompson

Essex County Council Libraries

First published in the UK 2008 by
A & C Black Publishing Ltd
38 Soho Square
London
W1D 3HB
www.acblack.com

Copyright © 2008 Blake Publishing
Published 2007 by Black Education Pty Ltd, Australia

ISBN: 978-1-4081-0512-2

A CIP catalogue record for this book is available from the British Library.

Written by Lisa Thompson and Elizabeth Dowen
Publisher: Katy Pike
Series Editor: Eve Tonelli
Cover Design: Terry Woodley
Designer: Rob Mancini
Printed in China by South China Printing Co. Ltd.

Cover image © Shutterstock

Illustration credits: p2 (ml), (mr), p4 (b), p9 (bl), (br), p24 (ml), (b), p25 (tr),
(ml), p26 (br), p29 (ml), p30 (br), p39 (tr), (ml), (mr), (b), p42 (bl), p43 (bl),
p44 (sl), p46 (b), p47 (tl)–Nahum Ziersch; p11 (ml), p16 (bm), (br), p17 (bl),
p27 (tm), (tr), (bl), (br), p28 (b)–Luke Mancini; p10 (bl), p11 (tr), p16, p20
(bl), p30, p36 (bl)–Shutterstock

This book is produced using paper made from wood grown in managed,
sustainable forests. It is natural, renewable and recyclable. The logging and
manufacturing processes conform to the environmental regulations of the
country of origin.

With grateful thanks to Mathew Mackareth from the Australian
Film Television and Radio School, Sydney, for his generous assistance
with this book.

All the Internet addresses given in this book were correct at the time of
going to press. The author and publishers regret any inconvenience caused
if addresses have changed or sites have ceased to exist, but can accept no
responsibility for any such changes.

Contents

And … action!   4

How I became an animator   8

A good animator   12

Who's who on the team?   14

The three stages of animation   18

Telling stories   20

Creating characters   28

Great moments in animation history   32

Tricks of the trade   34

Behind the scenes   38

The big night   43

Job opportunities   44

Useful contacts   46

Glossary   47

Index   48

And ... action!

Our latest project is a film!

I can sense my team's excitemen... as we gather for our first meeti... about this animation project. Andy, the director of a new sho... film, has brought us together to talk through the story so we ha... a clear picture of the movie he wants to make.

The team gets to work right away.

As the sequence supervisor in my team of five animators, it will be my job to make sure we stay on creative track and on schedule. The team has all read the script and we are now viewing the storyboard drawings pinned to the walls. Some of the team members have begun doing small sketches of characters and key scenes they'd like to do.

Louie- Tracking Shot

more speed desperate

clos...

Storyboards cov... the walls.

Louie. gasping, swiping?

Bish Extreme C-up

Hurrah! add cheering

4

We recently worked on an ad with dancing penguins!

It's an exciting time, yet also a little scary. My team and I normally work on creating animation for commercials or documentaries. This project has a lot more creative freedom.

Questions like 'How will certain scenes be created?' and 'What kind of techniques will we need to use?' swim around inside my head.

My mind is jumping from drawing mode to thinking about the technicalities of making this animation come to life.

That's one of the great things about computer-generated animation — you get to work at the cutting edge of technology and discover new ways to create animation.

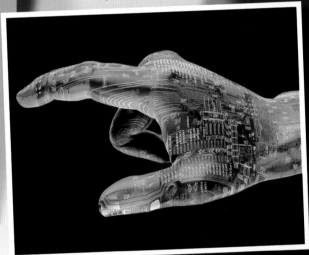

Start

My team and I are definitely ready to press 'start' and begin this adventure!

DID YOU KNOW?

Happy Birthday animation!
Humorous Phases of Funny Faces
by J. Stuart Blackton is generally considered to be the first ever animated film. The three-minute silent cartoon shows a hand drawing a man onto a chalkboard. A woman then appears too, and the characters take on a life of their own. It was made back in 1906, so animation has already celebrated its 100th birthday!

a couple of still images from the first-ever animated film

5

The meeting

Andy talks us through the story and explains how he imagines the finished film will look. We talk about the characters — their personalities, unique traits, motives, the places they visit and the world they live in. Then we look at the colours, lighting and camera angles for each scene.

Andy's vision for the film ...

helps us see how all the elements will work together.

There are lots of questions — we want as much information as possible so we can understand Andy's vision for the film. We leave the meeting feeling inspired and excited, armed with countless notes and clear ideas about the look and feel of the film.

OK, who's doing what?

Everyone's focused on the film.

It's my job to give key scenes and characters to each of my animators. Some of my team have already told me what they would like to work on. 'Animation' involves performing - the drawings and models replace actors and actresses, so I need to use the creative skills I learnt in drama and English.

ANIMATION TECHNIQUES

2D CEL ANIMATION

This is the most traditional form of animation. It involves sketching a picture by hand, turning the page and drawing the same picture in a slightly different position. The sketches are outlined in ink, filled in with colour and shot on film. An animator can also scan their drawings into the computer to turn pencil lines into black, inked lines. Then with a point of the cursor and a click of the mouse, the areas are filled in with colour.

That's a lot of sketching!

Here are the results.

STOP-MOTION ANIMATION

This style involves building small models, photographing them, making minor adjustments, and then photographing them again. It takes a tremendous amount of patience as 24–30 pictures create just one second of film or video and it can take up to 20 minutes to set up each shot.

examples of claymation models

CGI (COMPUTER GENERATED IMAGERY)

This involves sculpting shapes called polygons on the computer to build characters and scenes. An animator creates individual data for each character or object, including shading, texture, lighting and movements, to create a 3D image that can be manipulated to be seen from any angle.

DID YOU KNOW?

Computer animation has developed rapidly, thanks to advanced digital technology. The films *Over the Hedge*, *Shrek* and *The Incredibles* were made in this way, as well as CGI characters like Gollum in the *Lord of the Rings* and Yoda in the *Star Wars* films.

HOW I BECAME AN ANIMATOR

For as long as I can remember, I've loved drawing funny, little characters and making up stories about them. When I was five, I created a whole town of thumb-print characters and pages of comic strip adventures about them. There was even a superhero, Thumbman, and a little Princess Pinkie. We've all got to start somewhere!

I was always drawing, drawing, drawing.

This is Emerald the Fish.

This is my brother!

I practised by drawing myself too.

I almost got square eyes from watching cartoons!

I was forever trying to squeeze in time to watch one more cartoon before I went to school each morning. I'd save up my pocket money so I could see any new animated movie as soon as it came out.

ROAR!!

I still remember the first time I saw **The Lion King**. I was drawn into the world on the screen and the characters felt real to me. I loved the power of the story — its colour and energy. It was then that I knew I wanted to create characters that would come alive on screen too.

So, from around the age of eight, I started writing stories and keeping folders of all the characters I created. The stories and characters never really got much further than the folders (some never even made it that far), but creating them got my imagination working.

hard at work

what do you think of these?

I developed ideas and a passion for writing good stories. It also helped me understand what makes a good animated story and improved my drawing skills. Creating those folders started me on the road to becoming an animator.

He waits...

Deep in thought.

a voice calls out...

someone needs him!

He's coming!

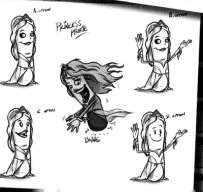

THUMBMAN.

A. OPTION

B. OPTION

C. OPTION

D. OPTION

A. OPTION

B. OPTION

PRINCESS PINKIE

C. OPTION

D. OPTION

BOING

I've polished some of my sketches for Thumbman and Princess Pinkie since then.

As I got older, I became interested in computers and began creating short animations on my computer. I'd scan in my drawings, and then add colour and sound. Through creating these little 2–5 minute animations, I learnt the basics of computer animation and how to use the software I needed. There are many animating software packages available which are relatively cheap and easy to use such as *Art Attack Comic Creator*, and *Kid Pix Studio Deluxe*.

He's got the right idea!

After I left school, I went to university, where I studied animation. My course included work experience so I worked at quite a few different companies - creating animations for the web, computer games, commercials and films - all whilst studying too. That was a busy time!

http://www

WWW

DVD

DIDYOUKNOW?

The first animated TV cartoon series was called *Crusader Rabbit*. It ran from 1949–1951.

I learnt so much at university.

Work experience gave me the chance to work on lots of different animations.

I was lucky enough to work with modellers, writers, directors and producers. That helped me understand what it is like to be part of a creative team — bouncing ideas off each other and coming up with new ways of doing things.

I worked on both 2D and 3D projects.

Computer animation technology is booming right now.

Working closely in a team gives you support and inspiration.

I've never stopped doodling.

My university qualification and work experience gave me a real advantage in finding a job after graduation. But, don't forget these jobs are highly sought after, so competition is tough — only about 3000 people work in animation in Britain and the studios tend to be very specialised and small. You need to be very determined but if you keep at it, and if you've got what it takes, the rewards can be great.

Most of the animation I create now is on computers, but I still enjoy creating new stories and drawing characters in pencil.

DIDYOUKNOW?

Animation is a popular area of film work, and UK animators are amongst the world-leaders. Just think of Aardman Animations' international success with *Wallace and Gromit*, *Chicken Run* and more recently, *The Curse of the Were Rabbit*.

A good animator—

- can draw well and has a flair for art
- Has good technical and ICT skills
- has an active, creative imagination and lots of original ideas
- understands how stories work
- has an eye for detail
- Has a flexible, adaptable approach to working – this job can involve handling both 3D models and computer programmes
- thinks creatively in both 2D and 3D
- is a visual problem solver
- can work to deadlines
- is prepared to do painstakingly detailed work
- can work both independently and as part of a team
- likes to keep learning (advances in animation software and programme are constant).

loves working with computers

PROBLEM

drawing skills

Learn

What does it mean?

ORIGIN 1950s: Fr...

animation n. 1

chiefly archaic

'Animation *noun*: 1. animated quality; liveliness; spirit; life.
2. the act of animating; act of enlivening.
3. the process of preparing animated cartoons.'

Our world of animation

Look around. Animation is everywhere!

- entertainment — movies, TV shows, documentaries, video and DVD games
- business — advertising, training videos, marketing and promotion
- science — teaching videos, research explanation and research projection
- medicine — research, training and investigation
- architecture — projections and design
- airlines — flight investigation and pilot training

See it before you build it — here's your house in 3D!

Animation helps scientists understand the human body better.

Things to remember about being an animator

Animation is time consuming. There are thousands of details involved in every shot. Whether it is a tiny movement of the eyes or a slight ripple of fur, an animator can tweak a single shot for weeks!

Projects can last from just a few days or weeks to make an advertisement, to months or even years when making a feature film. I enjoy this kind of project-based work since it means facing new challenges on a regular basis.

so many eyes to choose from

CHALLENGE!

13

Who's who on the team?

Putting an animation together is really a team effort, even though every member of the team usually works independently towards the common goal.

Sometimes you juggle multiple roles.

In small productions, animators may take on more than one role — in fact, they might take them all on!

If you look at the credits list at the end of any animation film or video, you will be surprised to see how many people are involved in its production. Jobs range from those at the development and pre-production stages, through to jobs carried out at the post-production stage. Jobs, and job titles, vary depending on the area of animation (computer animation, stop motion etc.).

The key roles when putting an animation together are:

Scriptwriter

Scriptwriters create the story and script for the animation. Writing for animation requires paying special attention to creating characters, scenes and settings that will work well visually. They work alongside a character designer and the actors who provide the live voice dialogues.

Director

The director is the creative leader of the film. They guide the whole team and ensure everyone is clear about the end result and the style and type of story that they are trying to tell.

Producer

The producer is the business leader of the film. It is their job to take care of budgets, schedules and contracts, as well as making sure the creative team is meeting all its deadlines. They work closely with the director to keep the project on time and on budget.

Art director

The art director is responsible for the look of the animation. Their job is to find the best possible way to tell the story. Good art direction always supports and reinforces the aims of the story and the characters.

Key animators

Using 2D animation, they provide the first drawings which are filled out and completed by assistants and 'in-betweeners'. In 3D animation, key animators work on screen to create and position the images.

Illustrator / Storyboard artist

To begin turning a story into animation, illustrators draw sketches to show the look and feel of the story. They develop key characters and action scenes so the plot can come to life visually.

Storyboard artists work with the director to break the story up into a series of scenes. They create storyboards which visually show how the scenes flow together so everyone involved has a clear picture of how the finished animation will look.

What is a storyboard?

A storyboard is a panel of sequenced sketches showing the scenes and action changes for an animation. They are used for movies, TV shows and even advertisements.

PULL OUT. (SHIPS FLY OV

CG (Computer Graphics) artist

CG artists build computer-generated versions of the characters and settings. Some artists may specialise in just one area — such as modelling, technical direction or lighting. There are also model-makers and animatronics specialists, who make the models, puppets and robotic characters.

Different stages of an animation include:

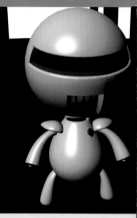

- creating the models (or skeletons) of the characters

- bringing the characte and settings to life by applying textures and movement to the model

Editor

Editors work with the director to make sure the pacing, timing and sound of the final animation work well together.

Composer / Sound director

Composers are responsible for all the music in an animation. They work closely with the sound director who arranges all the sound effects needed, like slamming doors and footsteps. The special effects animator can have an important role in adding a further dimension to the sound and imagery of the animation.

Compositor

Compositors bring together all the material, such as computer animation, special effects and live action, to create the final image.

• creating special
ffects and lighting so
looks as realistic as
ossible.

ON AIR

The longest-running animated TV programme is The Simpsons, which began in 1989 and is still on air today. It has been so successful, it also holds the title of the longest-running American sitcom.

17

THE ③ STAGES OF ANIMATION

① PRE - PRODUCTION
② PRODUCTION
③ POST - PRODUCTION

Timeline of how a CGI animation is created

1. Writers draft story into script form.

2. Script is read, discussed and finetuned.

3. Illustrators draw sketches of scenes and characters.

4. Storyboard artists create hundreds of storyboard drawings to map out story scene by scene.

5. Character voices recorded.

6. Character and background styles and looks chosen.

7. Storyboards put into final order and timed with characters' voices and other sounds to create animatics.

8. Modellers create computer models of characters, props and scenes.

9. Each computer model has a set of controls which determines how it will move — dozens of character files for movement and features created.

10. Background sets created in a rough blocked-out form.

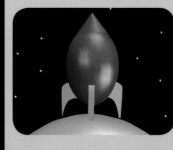

11. Animators add texture (like skin, fur and, hair) for each character.

12. Specific key poses created that dictate the movement of each character.

13. Special effects, like flowing water, lighting, shadows, weather elements and fire, added to both backgrounds and characters.

14. Rough animation finalised and signed off by director. Final 2D 'render' produced and given to post - production team.

15. Many individual animated layers that make up each shot flattened into final scene. This is called compositing.

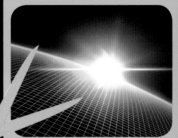

16. Editors cut final edit of film, making sure colour levels are correct for all scenes. Special effects finalised and any additional effects added if needed.

17. Volume levels for music, sound effects and dialogue balanced for best dramatic effect.

Telling stories

Once Upon a Time...

The first step for any animated film is getting the story right. Not all stories are suitable for animation. An animated story needs to have good visual potential.

Think about how the story would look in pictures.

Do you want to write a story for animation? Here are some story-building questions to ask yourself —

- What is the story about?
- How is the story told?
- Who is the hero?
- What does the hero want?
- Who or what is stopping the hero getting what they want?
- How does the hero achieve their goal (or not) in the end?

You need to understand what kind of story you are telling. A story could have one or more of the following themes:

- action
- quest
- romance
- good vs. evil
- mystery
- thriller
- tragedy
- comedy
- adventure
- science fiction

romance

mystery

science fiction

You also need to be clear about what action drives your story forward. For example, is it:

- to find something?
- to return home / be free?
- to break a spell?
- to get justice or revenge?
- to find love?
- to stop an evil villain?

Is there a hero?

Who's the villain in your story?

DIDYOUKNOW?

Animated hero

The most filmed cartoon character, Zorro, features in over 70 films and TV series. Created by Johnston McCulley, he was also the first comic-strip character to be the star in a major film, **The Mark of Zorro** (1920).

Writing a story for animation might sound easy, but it can take a long time, with many false starts and quite a few drafts to get it right.

THE END.

THE STORY BEHIND THE LION KING

Most people know that when *The Lion King* movie was released in 1994 it was an instant success – but what you might not know is that the story didn't come easily at all. Quite a few years before, there was just a vague idea to make a film about lions because one of the producers thought lions were cool!

Disney's writers tried different storylines and their artists created countless drawings of lions. They ended up with a story for a film called *King of the Beasts*. It was about a war between lions and baboons. Since Disney was already doing an animation called *Beauty and the Beast,* the film was retitled *King of the Jungle.*

The problem was that lions live in the savannah (open grasslands) – not the jungle. For the next few years, many story drafts went in the bin because no-one could quite work out what the story was about.

Eventually, a team of writers and animators took a trip to Africa. The trip was an inspiration and provided many ideas that made it into the final movie. When the team got back, they worked solidly for two weeks with the producer and the co-director.

They looked at all the information they had collected, took the story apart, figured out exactly who the characters were, what they wanted and what action would drive the story.

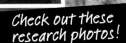

Check out these research photos!

Everyone went lion crazy when the movie came out!

Three years later, *The Lion King* finally reached the cinemas, became a smash hit around the world and proved how a little idea can become a great story – if you don't give up and do ask the right questions!

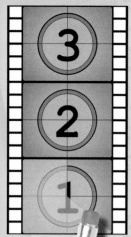

From STORY to SCRIPT to STORYBOARD

When a story is finalised, it is written into a script format. A script (or screenplay) contains not only the dialogue: it also describes the characters and their motivations, lists scene locations and includes stage directions.

These stage directions make up part of a script.

From the script, character sketches are drawn to see the look, feel, colour, lighting and mood of each character. Animators use these sketches as a guide when creating the characters on computers.

This is when characters come to life.

Meet Zoom.

Animation starts here!

Black and white sketches start off Zoom's storyboards.

Hundreds of these drawings map out the story in a visual way to create the storyboards. These quick sketches help plan the general placement of every camera shot and the action of the film.

The storyboard – the animation map

A storyboard looks like a comic book of the final film, showing all the significant shots and camera movements. It is the map that guides everyone through the production process. Artists and technicians must painstakingly produce every single frame in an animated film so they can get very detailed results.

Each one of these has to be individually filled with its own picture!

Opening shot

taking a look

Zoom spots spider

Close-up on web

Now, here's Zoom in his coloured board.

Once the storyboards reach a certain level of approval, a workbook is assembled from the key drawings. A workbook page contains panels from the storyboards with camera angles, technical information and descriptions of the action.

Storyboard to animatic

An editor adds rough voice recordings and sound to the storyboard frames to create an animatic (or storyboard animatic). Animatics help time the story and identify any areas that need tweaking.

a workbook being put together

lots of hours in front of the computer

Let's get the sound added!

WHAT IS AN ANIMATIC?

An animatic is created by editing together still images with a rough version of the soundtrack and running it in sequence. Animators use animatics to see if the sound and images are working well together. If there are any timing issues, changes are made to the storyboard or soundtrack. This avoids wasting time and money on animation that will not make the final cut.

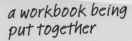

01:45

BREAKING THE STORY DOWN

The film is broken down into a series of sequences — the chase sequence, the fight sequence, the party sequence. Each sequence contains several individual scenes.

chase sequence

A scene is a continuous block of storytelling, either set in a single place or following a particular character. The end of a scene is typically marked by a change in location or time.

fight sequence

Maths for animators

Get ready for some maths.

To make an animation come to life, each second of film is broken down into 24 individual frames:

24 frames = 1 second of film.

Every action must be timed to look real and believable, so it is broken down into stages, for example, standing, sliding, falling, landing, recovering and standing up again. If this action is to last five seconds:

5 seconds x 24 frames a second = 120 frames are needed for this action.

Visually setting a scene

The director and the artists work out a series of rough drawings (the storyboards) that illustrate how every scene in a sequence will look. These drawings determine what we see, perspective and camera angles, if the scene zooms in or out of the path of action and lighting.

Rough sketches ...

turn into storyboards ...

which help us work out what we need to do for the final look of the animation.

After the storyboards are finalised, the director then works with our layout artists to generate a 3D animatic of the film. This allows much more precise planning for camera angles and lighting.

3D

Let's go 3D!

Where are we putting the shadows for this scene?

We use computers to create animated cinematography.

DIDYOUKNOW?

Animation around the world

A distinctive type of Japanese animation is called *anime*. Often inspired by Japanese *manga* (comics), these animations have a strong visual style and feature on television, DVDs and even computer and video games.

Manga animation has a style all its own.

a manga style drawing

27

When a character's look is decided upon, a character file is compiled that contains various eye, body and facial expressions. A single character may have hundreds of files of its features.

A few seconds of animation contains hundreds or thousands of moving parts and special features. An animator usually prepares an individual colour palette for each scene and each character.

Read her face. What is she saying?

I need a good eye for colour to get each character's look just right.

Ducky needs his own special shade of yellow.

Look who's talking!

Animators show characters' feelings through their hands, stance, mouth and eyes.

Cut
Copy
Create Shortcut
Delete

If you feed a computer the right information, it can save you a lot of work!

3D

In 3D computer animation, the animator works like a puppeteer. Each character model is manipulated by a series of commands that will create a performance. Unlike traditional hand-drawn or stop-motion (puppet) animation, the characters are not drawn or posed for every frame.

Instead, the animator sets up a series of key frames that specify when and where in a particular sequence a character will hold a certain pose and the computer will fill in the motion between each key frame.

Character tests

Before beginning to animate a character, an animator will usually test the model with some simple movement tests, such as a walk, a lip-sync test and an extreme pose test. This is to see where the character needs improvement and modification for movement.

Chuck, the superhero, in action!

As an animator, I need to be good at interpreting body language. Character animators are often thought of as the actors of animated film. It is my job to combine body movement and facial expressions to give each character an individual personality.

Trots, the pig, has buckets full of personality!

Much of what we think and feel is communicated not by words but through our eyes, hands, how we move and the way we use our bodies. Different body movements, gestures and facial expressions show a variety of feelings and meanings.

He looks crazy, but he's actually doing his research.

close-up research in action

Often, when I'm working out the look of a character, I will look at my own reflection in the mirror to see exactly how that emotion looks and the kind of message it is conveying.

To help us once we start animating, the characters' voices are recorded. It is important to do this early on in the process, so we can hear what each character sounds like. This will influence how we create the finer details of each character's look, behaviour and gestures.

Voice-over actors at work.

The voice-over artist experiments with many different voices and accents before the director decides on the right sound to match the look of each character.

A character's voice is so important that casting agents will spend time getting the right actors for an animation. Famous actors often work in animated films to provide memorable voices, like Mike Myers' Scottish accent for the ogre in Shrek.

Hmmm, whose voice would you pick for me?

How did they say that? How lip-syncing works...

Getting a character's mouth to move in time with the voice-over of the dialogue is known as lip-syncing. Different sounds need different mouth shapes. Speech is broken down into key sounds known as phonemes to capture these shapes.

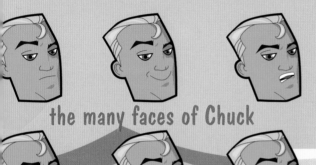

> The animation has to fit the sounds.

The animator must place the correct mouth shape at the right point in the animation so the character looks like they are making the right sound.

the many faces of Chuck

Once all the mouth shapes have been created for all the phonemes, they are placed in the character's file library.

PHONEMES

Here are a few examples of common phonemes you will recognise:

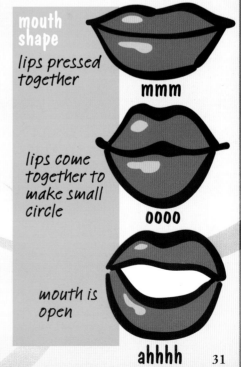

sound

mouth shape

lips pressed together

mmm

lips come together to make small circle

oooo

mouth is open

ahhhh

Great Moments in Animation History

Gertie the Dinosaur – one of the first animated cartoons

In 1913, an American artist called Windsor McCay drew 10,000 drawings on rice paper, then mounted them on cardboard and registered them as a film called *Gertie the Dinosaur*.

By working out most of the process himself, McCay painstakingly animated details like particles of dirt falling and water dripping. He gave Gertie personality and emotions. We see her eating, drinking, playing and even crying.

McCay is in Gertie's mouth in this frame!

In February 1914, *Gertie the Dinosaur* debuted as part of McCay's vaudeville act and was an instant success. At the end of the show, McCay would walk offstage and reappear as an animated figure in his own cartoon. The audience loved it. And that's how Gertie the dinosaur became the world's first animated star.

WINSOR McCAY'S "GERTIE"
WONDERFULLY TRAINED DINOSAURUS

WINSOR McCAY
AMERICA'S GREATEST CARTOONIST

GERTIE JUST LOVES AN AUTO.

Released through BOX OFFICE ATTRACTION CO
EXCHANGES IN ALL PRINCIPAL CITIES.

the original Gertie poster

CINEMA

TOY STORY

Animation in 3D – it's a whole new dimension!

Remember these guys from the movie?

Toy Story was all done on screen.

Toy Story was the first full-length movie animated entirely on computers. Animators worked over 800,000 hours on computers to get everything just right.

It took 70 animators to make the movie *Pocahontas* using traditional animation but only 27 animators to make *Toy Story* using computers – that's a big difference!

Fire & ICE

The animated movie *Ice Age* includes a scene where ice crumbles away around the characters to reveal a river of rapidly flowing lava. The scene is only on the screen for 185 seconds (4,441 frames) yet it took 15 technical directors more than 2,835 working hours and 22,579 lines of computer code to complete!

Who knew this could take so long to animate?

Hairy problem

Two of the most difficult things to create in CGI are fur and hair — it's hard making them look convincing and real.

These characters could do with some more work.

This kitten's a bit too fluffy!

Camera Magic

Distance from the camera

Different shots give the viewer different types of information:
- long shots (far away) show large amounts of information and set the scene
- medium shots bring you into the action
- close-ups and extreme close-ups show great emotion.

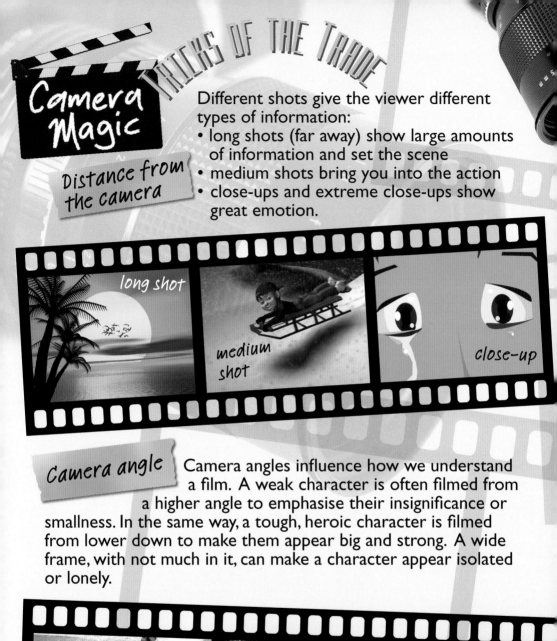

long shot

medium shot

close-up

Camera angle

Camera angles influence how we understand a film. A weak character is often filmed from a higher angle to emphasise their insignificance or smallness. In the same way, a tough, heroic character is filmed from lower down to make them appear big and strong. A wide frame, with not much in it, can make a character appear isolated or lonely.

Lens lingo

Film professionals describe camera movements with special terms, including:

- trucking in — camera moves towards an object
- panning — camera lens rotates from side to side whilst camera body remains in same position
- tilting — swinging the camera lens up and down on the spot
- jib or boom — to move the whole camera up and down
- tracking or dollying — moving the whole camera left or right.

Editing Magic

Pace

A lingering camera shot allows us to connect emotionally with characters, where fast cuts force us to constantly reassess the situation. Compare the average length of shots in a fight or action sequence to an emotional scene. You'll find action shots are short and snappy, and emotional scenes use fewer and longer shots.

Image sequence

The way images are arranged tells us about settings and emotions. Editors have the power to put shots into a different order from the storyboard, or even cut out whole sequences — massively changing not only the feel of the story but the actual story itself.

In animation, the editor makes the most savage cuts at the 2D/3D animatic stage — otherwise, we animators could waste our time creating something that will just end up on the cutting room floor.

How motion capture works

In motion capture (or mo-cap as we say in the industry), optical or magnetic markers are placed on the actor's major joints. They then perform the desired movements whilst wearing these markers. A series of cameras or magnets, carefully placed around the stage, record the magnet information from all these joints onto a computer.

The recorded motion of the actor's joints is mapped onto the CG character's joints. This means the animated character is a combination of the movements of the actor and the computer-generated character.

Through the magic of mo-cap, Alex, the actor becomes ...

Arthur, the CG accountant!

The makers of computer and video games are the biggest users of mo-cap, which helps them create realistic characters for their games.

If you've played games, you've probably already been watching mo-cap in action!

DID YOU KNOW?

MO-CAP MOVIES

The 2006 film **Monster House** used 3D motion-capture techniques to digitally record the physical performances of all the actors. A fully animated movie, populated by all those actors' characters, was created from the dialogue and motion capture information — amazing!

This is how they map the image.

Special Effects

Almost all movies we see today have some kind of CGI special effect in them, whether it is to make a natural element look more dangerous, like fire, smoke or clouds, or it is a whole character or background.

The mist is a special effect to give the image more impact.

These entire characters were created by special effects.

Special effects animators often rely on computer programmes to recreate how things look and act in the real world — like clouds swirling, or a rock being dropped and bouncing.

special effects animation in the rough

This is how they used to do horror make-up! Our industry often uses computer special effects now.

They then see where and when they need to add their enhancements. Or even add a completely different effect, like a flash of light or a puff of smoke, that would not naturally occur but would look believable.

Computer programs calculate how to make animated water ripples look realistic.

Behind the Scenes

After the meeting

CREW ONLY

Many hours later, I gather my team together to let them know what characters and scenes they will be working on. I give each animator their own allocated scene list and one major character and one or two minor characters.

My major character is a crocodile named Louie, and my minor ones are a pair of swamp flies called Bisk and Ed. Time to do some research!

You're doing this, and you're doing that — hope everyone's ok with that?

Research

File Edit

New...
Open...
Open As...
Open Rece

starting the animation process

Now we all know our characters and scenes, we individually set to work over the coming months to bring them to life. We work with the modellers and technical directors to build character and scene colour palettes — and apply texture and create character files.

All the while, we must follow the technical specifications of each scene and setting as outlined in the workbook.

Here's Louie!

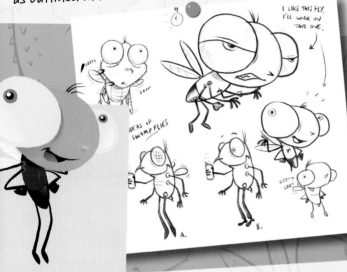

I play around with Louie, trying to get his personality and little unique traits just right. I pay particular attention to his eyes, snout and tail.

I do the same with Bisk and Ed. It is important to experiment with all the characters until you know how they would look in any situation and with any reaction.

I create model sheets for each character so I have a quick reference guide for how they look wearing basic expressions — like happy, surprised, normal, scared, or excited.

a print out of one of Louie's model sheets

Once each of the characters is modelled and has texture applied, I begin to run through movement sequences with each one.

FLIP BOOK DAILY MEETINGS

Each animator produces a daily flip book. This is a low-resolution version of their work. A flip book can be anything from a group of key character frames to an almost completed scene.

The editors then add sound to all the books and put them into sequence. The team, along with Andy, views the work to see where we're up to and if anything needs tweaking.

Everybody gather round, please.

Piece by piece, the animation comes together. The studio becomes a busy hive of activity as we work hard to create our characters and scenes — and stay on top of our deadlines!

time to view the day's work

Lynne and Sam (technical directors) hard at work!

DID YOU KNOW?

In the last twenty years, British animators have become famous worldwide. Nick Park won an Oscar for *Creature Comforts* in 1989. The success of this and the *Wallace and Gromit* films, *A Grand Day Out*, *The Wrong Trousers* and *A Close Shave*, encouraged DreamWorks to co-produce the feature-length animation *Chicken Run*.

FRIDAY SCREENINGS

Every Friday, the editors put together the whole week's work and we have a screening so the entire team — director, producer, animators, modellers etc. — can see how it's looking.

Each week, the screenings get more and more exciting as the characters and scenes become more complete.

THE DEADLINE DRAWS NEAR

A4 5·B6 12
FILM THIS
B.I. GTIME
GWHIZ
3/6/10

Weeks turn into months. The days get longer and the nights get later as we rush to meet deadlines. We begin to talk about our characters as if they really do exist.

You have good days and bad days with your characters, just as if they are real. I chat to the other animators about my characters and what they're doing, and the other animators do the same.

I begin to realise I am spending more time with Louie, Bisk and Ed than I am with my real friends! It's getting weird, but I know the end is near!

DIDYOUKNOW?

Time to flip out

A flip book contains a series of pictures that change gradually from one page to the next, so when you turn the pages quickly, the pictures appear to change or move.

Now, there are software packages and websites that convert digital video files into custom-made computer flip books.

The first ever flip book was created in 1868 by John Barnes Linnet and called a kineograph (which means moving picture).

The final countdown

Some scenes are ready to have their special effects added and are almost complete.

Individually, we show our work to Andy and the editor, and make any final adjustments. Often, we just need to tweak the lighting or add minor elements or props.

This is where computers are perfect for something as time consuming as animation. Changes that would take days to redraw by hand in traditional cel animation, we can do much quicker now by pressing a few keys on a keyboard.

Thanks to computers, we can work so much faster.

Finally, we hand everything over to the post – production team. All we can do now is wait.

THE BIG NIGHT

The first screening of the finished animation

I don't think Louie would approve, but I'm wearing the best crocodile skin shoes I could find! The team are wearing T-shirts featuring their characters.

I love going to premieres!

It has been just over two years since our first meeting with Andy. Now, finally, it is the moment of truth — we are going to see the end result of all our hard work.

The lights go down, the music begins and there on the screen is the world my team and I helped bring to life. Suddenly, I see Louie race across the screen, with Bisk chasing close behind.

This is it!

It's so exciting. I loved creating that scene. Everyone laughs as Bisk crosses the line first. My heart jumps with pride. One by one, the team get to see their characters and scenes on the big screen.

It looks even better than I imagined!

I love the way the final movie looks.

Weeks of work flash by in seconds, months of work flash by in minutes. It's such a thrill for us to see how wonderful it looks and know that we've achieved so much.

Even though we know the story inside out, we don't even want to blink — we don't want to miss a frame. It's like meeting up with old friends — to us, our characters really have come to life!

APPLAUSE

Wow, fantastic! It was worth all the hard work.

43

Follow these steps to become an animator

1

At school, studying art and design, and/or 3D effects and model making will start you in the right direction. Develop your design skills through computer programmes if possible. About 80% of those working in the industry hold degree-level qualifications.

find your arty side

2

To take a degree in animation, you usually need supporting GCSEs and:

- two A levels (one may need to be in an art- or media-related subject), or
- the Diploma in Creative and Media (a new qualification available from September 2008), or
- a relevant BTEC National qualification, or
- an art Foundation course.
- It's important to check individual course entry requirements carefully.

love your computer

3a

There are a range of degree courses, Higher National Diplomas and foundation degrees that specialise in animation and related subjects, including computer animation. Many more higher-education institutions offer art and design courses that include an animation studies element. Check the content of different courses - some are very technical, others more creative. You need to decide what sort of course best matches your interests and skills. Skillset (the Sector Skills Council for the audio visual industries) currently accredits six degree-level animation courses at various universities. More information is on the Skillset website (see page 47).

3b

If you decide to do a more general art and design degree you may be able to specialise through a postgraduate course. You can search for courses of any level in animation (and in other media-related subjects) in the BFI/ Skillset Media Courses Directory, which can be accessed online through the animation section of Skillset's website. You can also, of course, search for foundation degree, HND and degree courses on the UCAS website: www.ucas.com

Opportunities for animators

- animatic artist — producing animatics for film projects
- film animator — animating for both short films and feature-length movies
- game designer — creating video or computer game animation
- web designer — making online services fun and interesting
- visual effects artist — focusing on effects animation
- broadcast graphics designer — creating titles and animations for television stations
- architectural visualisation — making model houses come to life!

Competition for jobs is quite stiff, as animation has become a highly popular area in which to train. Many of the new jobs are in the creation of computer games. Around half of those in the industry work on a freelance basis, undertaking projects on short-term contracts, as work becomes available with different organisations.

DIDYOUKNOW?

You could create animation for TV.

Starting salaries in animation studios are around £14-20,000. Senior animators might expect to earn around £25,000, rising to over £40,000 for very successful and experienced animators.

Get creative!

http://www

Want to work online?

OTHER RELATED CAREER AREAS TO CONSIDER:

- ## Cartoonists

Cartoons are found in newspapers, magazines, comics and illustrated books. Cartoonists don't need formal qualifications, although art training may help - such as a degree in graphic design and illustration or animation.

- ## Special effects

UK special effects work has an excellent reputation worldwide. Much of the work is computerised, but also involves creative ideas and artistic and technical skills. There are opportunities for people with qualifications at all levels, although many entrants are graduates. There are only around 650 special effects personnel in the UK film industry.

- ## Film making

Thousands of people work in film and video in the UK. An increasing number of roles in this area are now concerned with digital technology.

- ## Website design and management

Generally speaking, website designers create the look of websites, website developers are concerned with the more technical aspects of the design and website managers maintain them.

Useful contacts

Skillset - Prospect House, 80-110 New Oxford Street, London WC1A 1HB. Tel: 020 7520 5757. The Sector Skills Council for the audio visual industries. For advice, call the free media careers helpline on 08080 300 900. *www.skillset.org/careers www.skillset.org/animation*

BFI (British Film Institute) - Education Unit, 21 Stephen Street, London W1T 1LN. Tel: 020 7957 4787. Look on the education section of the BFI website for information about events for a searchable course database. *www.bfi.org.uk/learn.html*

National Media Museum - Bradford, West Yorkshire BD1 1NQ. Tel: 0870 70 10 200. Formerly the National Museum of Photography, Film and Television. Offers short animation workshop courses for students.

Creative and Cultural Skills and **learndirect** run a specialist helpline for people working in or wanting to work in the arts. You can phone free on 0800 093 0444.

BECTU (Broadcasting Entertainment Cinematograph and Theatre Union)- 373-377 Clapham Road, London SW9 9BT. Tel: 020 7346 0900.

Animation Directory 2007 - annual directory listing UK animation companies

The Knowledge 2007 Includes details of film, television, video and commercials production companies. Also see: www.animationuk.com

Glossary

2D (2 Dimensional) — having two dimensions, for example, length and width

3D (3 Dimensional) — having three dimensions, for example, length, width and depth

camera angle — specific location at which a camera is placed to take a shot, for example, high, low etc.

cel — hand-drawn sheet representing a single animation frame

code — instructions given to a computer to perform a function; written in a programming language, for example, JavaScript

compositing — creating complex images or moving images by combining images from different sources, for example, digital video or film, 2D animations, painted backdrops, digital still photographs and text

frame — single photographic image bordered by frame lines and traditionally in strips contained in reels

manipulated — changed or controlled skillfully

optical — relating to light

production — process by which a film is created; something that is produced

scene — continuous block of storytelling, either in a single place or following a single character

sequence — continuous or connected series

special effects — effects used to produce scenes that cannot be achieved by normal or natural methods (especially on film)

storyboard — series of illustrations in sequence to visually show a story; looks like a large comic strip; used to spot any problems before production begins

trait — distinguishing feature of someone's personality, for example, sense of humour

vaudeville — popular theatre entertainment in America from 1880s–1920s, featuring a variety of acts, for example, music or comedy

visual potential — possibly able to be communicated interestingly in a visual format, for example, cartoon, film

voice-over artist — professional actor who provides the offscreen voice for characters or narration in any media, for example, television, film, radio

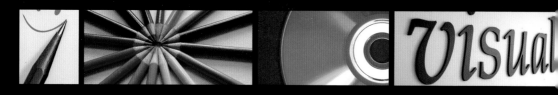

Index

2D	7, 12, 19, 35
3D	7, 12, 27, 28, 35, 36
animator	4, 6, 7, 9, 12–14, 19, 23–26, 28, 29, 31, 33, 35, 37, 38, 40, 41, 44, 45
artist	16, 18, 22, 25, 27, 30, 34, 45
camera	6, 25, 27, 32, 34–36
cartoon	5, 8, 12, 17, 21, 32
CG	7, 16, 18, 33, 36, 37
colour	6–8, 10, 19, 24, 28, 38
director	4, 11, 15–17, 19, 23, 27, 30, 33, 38, 40, 41
draw	4, 5, 7–12, 16, 18, 22, 24, 25, 27, 28, 34, 42, 44
editor	17, 19, 25, 35, 40–42
film	4–7, 10, 13, 15, 19–22, 24–27, 29, 30, 32, 34–36, 45
games	10, 13, 27, 36, 45
lighting	6, 7, 16, 17, 19, 24, 27, 42
model	7, 11, 16, 18, 28, 29, 38, 39, 41
music	17, 19, 43
producer	11, 15, 22, 23, 41
scene	4–7, 14, 16, 18, 19, 24, 26–28, 33–35, 38–43
story	4, 6, 8, 9, 11, 14–16, 18, 20–26, 33, 35, 43
script	4, 14, 18, 24
setting	14, 16, 27, 35, 39
software	10, 12, 41
sound	10, 17–19, 25, 30, 31, 40
special effects	19, 37, 42
TV	13, 16, 17, 21
writer	11, 14, 18, 22, 23